MUSEUMS

GREAT PLACES TO VISIT

Jason Cooper

The Rourke Corporation, Inc.
Vero Beach, Florida 32964

Edited by Sandra A. Robinson

PHOTO CREDITS
© Lynn M. Stone: All photos except page 10, © the Smithsonian Institution

LIBRARY OF CONGRESS
Library of Congress Cataloging-in-Publication Data
Cooper, Jason, 1942-
   Museums / by Jason Cooper.
   p. cm. — (Great places to visit)
   Includes index.
   Summary: An introduction to the variety of museums that exist and the many pleasures they contain.
   ISBN 0-86593-209-3
   1. Museums—United States—Juvenile literature. [1. Museums.]
I. Title. II. Series: Cooper, Jason, 1942- Great places to visit.
AM11.C65 1992
069'.0973—dc20   92-12556
                              CIP
                              AC

TABLE OF CONTENTS

MUSEUMS

Where can you see old pictures and planes, mummies and mountain goats, statues and snakes? Where can you see bones and birds, coins and cars, tigers and tyrannosaurs? In **museums,** of course.

Museums are places that keep and show, or **exhibit,** many things of interest and importance.

Each museum's **collection**—the objects it shows—is different. Each museum is full of exciting, sometimes amazing, surprises.

Tyrannosaur skeleton

ART MUSEUMS

People visit art museums to see paintings, statues, pottery, jewelry, weapons, **carvings** and many other objects. Artists make carvings by cutting and shaping such things as wood, marble and ivory.

In a big art museum, you can travel back through time just by moving from one room to another. Each room holds art treasures from another time.

Lion guards the Art Institute of Chicago

SCIENCE MUSEUMS

Science museums have lifelike exhibits that show nature as it is now and as it may have been long ago.

In science museums you can see many kinds of animals and their **habitats,** the kinds of places where they live.

Some kinds of animals exhibited in the museum may be **extinct**—they no longer exist. Bones of extinct dinosaurs, for example, are popular exhibits in many science museums.

Visiting a lifelike habitat exhibit

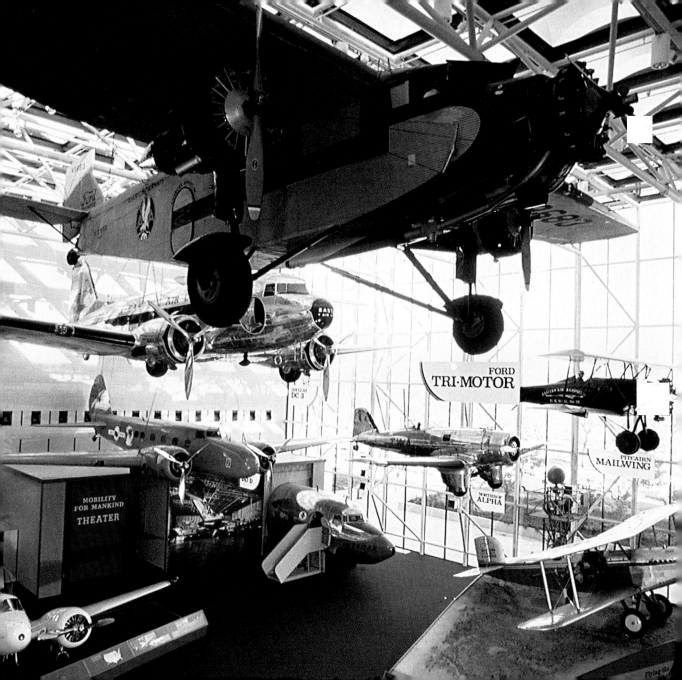

MUSEUMS WITH MACHINES

Some museums have cars, trains or airplanes, the machines that transport people.

Railroad museums show steam engines and other locomotives that hauled trains in the past.

The National Air and Space Museum in Washington, D.C., exhibits old planes and American spacecraft.

At the Museum of Science and Industry in Chicago you can walk aboard another unusual machine—a German submarine from World War II.

Ford Trimotor and other aircraft at the National Air and Space Museum, part of the Smithsonian Institution, Washington, D.C.

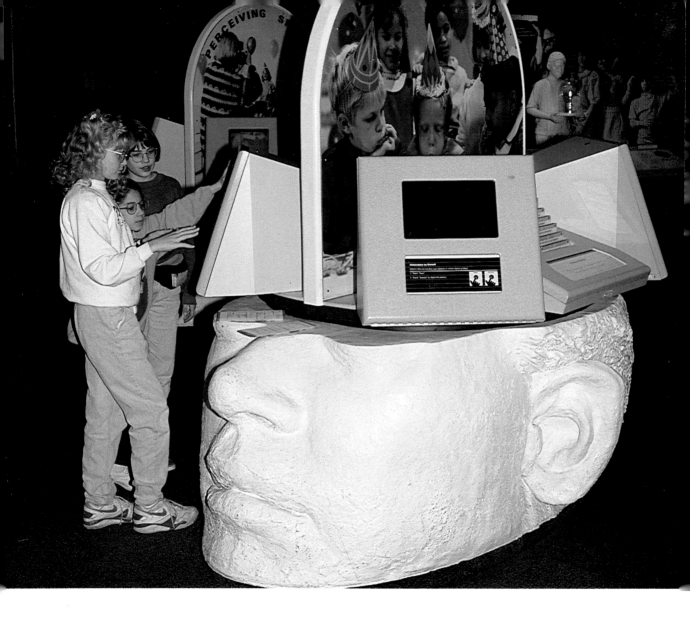

Exploring how the human brain works in a hands-on exhibit

Railway museums display old locomotives

CHILDREN'S MUSEUMS

If you want to learn and have fun—children's museums are great places. The science, math, music, history, computer and art exhibits are often "hands-on." That means you don't have to just look. You can touch, too!

Some children's museums have collections of dolls, doll houses, model trains and toys.

A walk-through "heart" at the Museum of Science and Industry, Chicago

SPECIAL MUSEUMS

A museum may be limited to a single, special interest. It could be a baseball, basketball, police or fire fighter's museum. It could also be a cultural museum for a particular group, such as African Americans, Hispanics or Native Americans.

Living museums are usually old-style (historic) villages with actors who dress, behave and talk like the people who would have lived there.

Artist George Catlin's painting of Osceola, at the Seminole Museum in Florida

BEHIND THE EXHIBITS

On your visit to the museum, you may meet one of the skillful people who works there.

Some members of the museum staff locate new objects. Others study the museum's collections or prepare them for exhibits.

Museum workers make up educational programs, raise money for the museum and plan exhibits.

Museum artists and writers make the exhibits more colorful and useful to visitors.

Field Museum artist Peggy McNamara at the snow leopard exhibit

MUSEUMS AS TEACHERS

You will learn something from your visit to a museum. You may learn from just looking at the exhibits and reading about them. But many museums help people learn by offering programs with guest speakers, fine films and hands-on exhibits. A museum may also provide guided tours.

Museum gift shops have books, toys, video tapes and other educational materials for sale.

Museum teacher displays penguin feathers for young visitors

MUSEUM TREASURES

Museums keep rare, unusual and beautiful objects. Many museum pieces are worth hundreds of thousands of dollars. This is why you may see a uniformed guard in each room of a museum.

Many items in a museum could never be replaced if they were lost or stolen.

If you have a collection at home, maybe it will be valuable and wind up in a museum some day.

Glossary

carving (KAHR ving) — object that has been made by an artist using sharp tools

collection (kuhl EK shun) — the group or groups of objects kept by a museum

exhibit (ex IHB it) — a museum object and its surroundings; the act of showing an object (to exhibit something)

extinct (ex TINKT) — no longer existing

habitat (HAB uh tat) — the kinds of places animals live, such as forests or deserts

living museum — (LIH ving mu ZEE uhm) a collection, usually of buildings, in which actors recreate the past

museum (mu ZEE uhm) — a place and organization that keeps and shows important collections of objects

INDEX